Great Escapes
of the Bible

Clio Turner

Illustrated by Beccy Blake

Many people in the Bible had to escape from danger for one reason or another. Their stories are very exciting!

Scripture Union

By the same author:
Hidden Heroes Of The Bible

© Clio Turner 2000
First published 2000
Reprinted 2002

Scripture Union, 207–209 Queensway, Bletchley,
Milton Keynes, MK2 2EB, England.
Email: info@scriptureunion.org.uk
Website: www.scriptureunion.org.uk
ISBN 1 85999 433 4

British Library Cataloging-in-Publication Data.
A catalogue record of this book is available from the
British Library.

Printed and bound in Great Britain by
Creative Print and Design (Wales) Ebbw Vale.

Scripture Union is an international Christian charity
working with churches in more than 130 countries,
providing resources to bring the good news about Jesus
Christ to children, young people and families and to
encourage them to develop spiritually through the Bible
and prayer.

As well as our network of volunteers, staff and associates
who run holidays, church-based events and school
Christian groups, we produce a wide range of
publications and support those who use our resources
through training programmes.

Contents

These stories come from a part of the Bible called the Old Testament. That means they happened a very long time ago! They have been re-told in modern English. We hope that you enjoy them.

Chapter One

Rahab and the spies

A very long time ago, God was leading his special people, the Israelites, into a new land. It was an exciting time but it was also quite scary. The people who already lived in the new land did not believe in God. They did not want the Israelites to take over. So the Israelites knew that they would have to fight for every little bit of the land.

The first big city in this new country was called Jericho. It was well guarded and it had very high walls! The leader of the Israelites was a man called Joshua. He decided not to attack the city straight away, but to send in spies. The spies could have a careful look round and tell Joshua where the city was weak.

The two spies got into the city, late in
the afternoon. It was a frightening time for
them. They had to pretend to be local
people, but of course they didn't know
their way around.

The spies did not want people to hear their Israelite voices.

They pushed on through the narrow, dusty streets until they came to a house which looked more welcoming than the rest. They had to stop somewhere, so one of the men plucked up courage and knocked on the front door.

The woman who came to the door was called Rahab.

So they went inside. But their problems were not over. The King of Jericho had already heard a rumour that spies were inside his city.

"Quick!" he shouted. "I want every house searched!"

When the searchers got to Rahab's house, she went to the door. "Yes, I did see two strange men," said Rahab. "But they left some time ago. They did not say where they had come from. I think they headed out of the city. If you hurry, you might catch them!"

The king's soldiers believed everything Rahab said. They set off out of the city right away, looking for the men. Then the city gates closed for the night.

But Rahab went upstairs to her roof...

Rahab explained that she wanted to help the two men because she thought they were on the winning side!

"We have all heard the stories about your God and how marvellous he is," she said. "We are terrified because the real God is on your side. We do not stand a chance. We know that you are bound to win and that this city will fall into your hands."

This cheered up the spies.

Then Rahab said, "I have looked after you. Will you do the same for me? I will show you a way to escape the city now and send you safely on your way. Will you promise that when you attack our land you will not hurt my family or me?"

The spies promised. But they told Rahab what she must do.

"You *must* tie this red rope to the window of your house," they said. "And you *must* make sure that all your family are inside when we come to attack your city. That way we will know where you all are and we will make sure that you are safe. If any of your family go outside, they may be killed in the fighting."

"I will do exactly as you say," said Rahab. Then she said, "I will trust you and I will learn to trust your God."

Then came the most scary bit of the whole day for the spies. The city gates were shut so they could not leave that way. But Rahab's house was part of the city wall. That meant that one side of the house faced out towards the open country.

Rahab took the red rope and they went to a small window on that side of the house. The window was just big enough for the spies to squeeze through. The spies looked out. It was a very long way down!

"I'm sure you will be all right!" said Rahab. "After all, God has looked after you so far." She tied the rope around the waist of one of the men.

It was a very tricky operation. But before long, both spies were standing safely on the ground outside the city wall.

They waved to Rahab and ran off into the night.

The two spies went back to their commander, Joshua, with some exciting news.

They said, "The city is strong but the hearts of its people are weak! The people

are all so frightened of our God that we are
sure to win!"

And they were right. Joshua's victory
over Jericho is one of the most famous
stories in the Bible.

Rahab and her family were kept safe by
Joshua and his men. Rahab settled down
among God's people and she became very
happy. She even married a man from
Israel, whose name was Salmon.

**If you want to find out more about
Rahab and the spies, their story can
be found in Joshua, chapter 2.**

Chapter Two

David the runaway

David ran home in a panic!

Quick, quick! The King is after me. He's very angry.

"What?" cried Michal, his wife. She was very upset by David's news. Michal knew only too well how frightening it was when the king was angry. After all, she was the king's daughter!

But this time, it was worse than Michal expected.

"He tried to kill me!" David said.

"But why – what have you done wrong?" Michal asked.

"Nothing!" said David. " It's what I've done *right* – not what I've done *wrong* that's the problem. I think the king's angry with me because I've been more successful in battle than he has."

"Oh help!" said Michal as she followed David inside and to their upper room. "Oh help!" she said again as she sat down on their bed.

David was one of King Saul's chief servants. He was also a captain in his army. David was so successful in battle that he had been allowed to marry Princess Michal as a reward.

But secretly, King Saul was never pleased with David. In fact he was *jealous* of him. That made matters worse.

The more battles David won, the more jealous King Saul became. In the end he hated David.

When David came back from the wars, the local people made him their hero rather than the king.

So, the better David did, the more trouble he got into!

David thought back to that afternoon.

"It was awful!" he said to his wife Michal. "I was playing music for the king. It usually soothes him when he's in a bad temper. I thought the king seemed to like it. I thought he was falling asleep. Then, all of a sudden..."

"The spear went into the wall!" said David. "And I had to run for my life just to get here. I'm sure our house is being watched by the king's soldiers. Whatever will we do now?" he asked his wife.

Michal sat very still and thought for a minute. "Somehow, we've got to get you out of here," she said.

Then Michal jumped up suddenly. "I know what!" she said. "We'll wait until it's dark. That way nobody can see what we're doing. They are bound to be watching the front door. But we can get you out through the back window!"

"What?" said David. He was horrified! "Isn't it a long way down?" he said.

"Not really!" said Michal. "It's our only hope. Just think. Tomorrow morning, when my father sends his soldiers in here for you, you'll be *miles* away."

David gulped, but he decided to give it a go.

So, as soon as it was dark...

As soon as David was safely on the ground he ran as fast as he could into the bushes. No-one had seen him!

Michal set to work upstairs with the second part of the plan. She got together some old clothes and other bits and pieces which they had in the house. Then...

Sure enough, next morning, Saul's soldiers arrived.

"We've come for David. Where is he?" asked the chief soldier.

Michal stood in the doorway. "I'm sorry. He can't come with you now. He is ill!" she said.

The soldiers went straight back to the king. But King Saul was not easily put off. "Bring him to me, even if he is ill," he roared. "If I have to, I will kill him in his bed!"

So the soldiers returned to David's house. But when they tried to get him from his bed...

...David wasn't there.

The king was very angry. He sent for Princess Michal.

"Why have you lied to me, my daughter?" he cried out.

"David *made* me do it," she replied.

But of course by this time, David was far, far away.

If you want to know more about David, his story starts in 1 Samuel, chapter 16.

Chapter Three

Elijah gets a strange menu

There was once a very wicked king in Israel called Ahab. He told the Israelites to forget all about God. But a good man, called Elijah, took no notice of the king. Elijah prayed to God every day and he was eager to do exactly what God wanted.

One day, God sent Elijah to the king with a very strange message...

The king was horrified and very angry.

But because God had told Elijah what to say, his words came true. The rain stopped. The grass withered. The flowers wilted. And the fruit fell from the trees.

While all this was happening, Elijah had to run for his life. As you can imagine, he was not very popular with the king. God told Elijah to run a long way out into the country and up into the hills. There was a little stream there that had not dried up yet.

"I will keep you safe here," said God. "King Ahab will never find you."

Elijah looked around him. He could see why the king would never think of looking for him there. It was a strange place. The valley floor was narrow and rocky. There were no trees. There were no shrubs. Elijah looked at the little stream. "At least I'll have plenty to drink," he thought. "But what am I going to do for food?"

"Leave it to me!" said God. "I have a plan."

God's plan was stranger than Elijah could have expected.

That evening, as Elijah was just getting ready to lie down, a flock of huge black birds swooped down into the valley.

The birds were ravens. And when Elijah looked at what they were throwing at him, he found that it was bread and meat! The birds did the same thing the next morning... and the next night.

The ravens kept bringing food, day after day. It wasn't very interesting living in the little valley. But at least Elijah was safe and well fed!

Then one day the little stream dried up. There had not been any rain for a long time.

"What's going to happen now?" said Elijah.

"Don't worry," said God, "Here is the second part of my plan! Go to the little town of Zarephath that is just outside Israel. You will meet a poor woman when you come to the town gates. I will use her to take care of you. And I will use you to take care of her!"

This sounded very strange to Elijah. But he did what God said. He hurried off to the town of Zarephath, being very careful to keep out of the way of the King Ahab.

Elijah went to the town gate and sure enough...

Elijah was pleased when he saw what the woman was doing. "She's going to make a fire," he thought. "Hooray. I'm desperate for some hot food."

But when he went up to talk to the woman, Elijah found that things were not quite as they seemed.

I'm sorry. I haven't any food to spare.

The woman explained that she had only enough food left for one last meal. Because the rain had stopped, all the crops had stopped growing.

"My son and I are about to die," said the woman. "A handful of flour and a few drops of oil are all we have left in the world!"

But Elijah was not put off. He remembered what God had said.

He said to the woman, "If you will share your last food with me, I promise that the flour and oil in your house will not run out until the day God sends rain again."

The woman looked into Elijah's eyes. What he was saying did not make sense, but she believed him. So she took Elijah home to stay with her and her son.

There was only a little flour and a little oil in the house each day. But when they came to make food there was always enough to go round.

God kept Elijah safe there until the time came for the rain to start again.

If you want to find out more about Elijah, the ravens and the widow, their story can be found in 1 Kings, chapter 17.

Chapter Four

Joash, the boy king

Things went from bad to worse for God's people. Many of their rulers led them the wrong way. Sometimes God was forgotten. Sometimes God was disobeyed on purpose.

One of the worst rulers of all was a woman called Athaliah. Athaliah was a daughter of Ahab, the evil king in the last story. Athaliah hated God and she hated anybody who got in her way.

People were frightened of Athaliah. Nobody dared to stand up against her.

Although Athaliah was really only the queen mother, her son the king did *everything* that she wanted. Athaliah had the kingdom in her grip.

Then one day, the king was murdered.
But instead of being upset, Athaliah was
just cross.

"What if I lose my power?" she
thought. "If my son is not the king,
perhaps no one will listen to me any
more."

Then Athaliah came up with a dreadful
plan.

"I will kill all my grandchildren," she
decided. "Then no-one will be able to rule
except me."

And she set about doing just that.

One of the grandchildren was a baby boy called Joash. When his aunt heard about the queen mother's plan, she ran quickly to the baby's bedroom.

Quick, quick! We must hide the baby prince.

The prince's aunt did not have time to explain. She grabbed the hand of the nurse. "You must trust me," she said. "Someone is coming to hurt the prince!"

The nurse did not need to be told twice. She picked up the baby and ran for the door.

The aunt knew of an old bedroom in the Temple that was not being used any more. It was a safe place to hide.

Joash's aunt explained that her husband was a priest. "He lives and works in the Temple," she said. "I'm sure that the baby will be safe if he comes and lives with us there."

That sounded good to the nurse. So she bundled Joash under her cloak and crept out of the palace with his aunt. It was very cold out in the night air, but the baby didn't cry at all. He was fast asleep, snuggled up to his nurse.

Soon they arrived at the Temple where the priest was waiting for them. "You'll be safe with me," he said. And sure enough, they were.

When evil Queen Athaliah stormed into Joash's room, there was no baby there. His aunt had rescued him just in time.

Joash grew up in the temple and nobody knew that he was really a prince. Joash's nurse, his aunt and his uncle the priest kept the secret. The Temple was so big that there were plenty of places to hide.

Athaliah ruled the land and the people hated her. No-one dared argue with the queen. But in the Temple, the priest taught Joash many things about God and Joash asked lots of questions.

Tell me about God, Uncle.

At last the day came when the priest decided it was time to bring Joash out of hiding. He was going to explain to the people that Joash was their true king. By now, Joash was seven years old.

The priest had a plan to make sure that Joash would be safe even when people found out who he was. First of all, he told all the leaders of the army that the boy living in the Temple was the real king. The leaders of the army travelled throughout the land and told all the leaders of the people. Then they came back to Jerusalem and waited until the Sabbath day. The army leaders gathered in the Temple ready for battle.

Joash was brought out and the army gathered round him to keep him safe. The people cheered and the priest put a crown on his head. "This is the real king," he shouted.

The trumpeters blew their trumpets. The people clapped and cheered loudly. "Hooray!" they called.

Up in her palace Athaliah heard all the noise and the cheering. She rushed to the Temple...

Athaliah was too late. The boy king had already been crowned and Athaliah had lost her kingdom!

If you want to find out more about King Joash, his story can be found in 2 Kings, chapters 11 and 12.

These stories come from a part of the Bible called the New Testament. That means they happened around the time of Jesus, about 2000 years ago!

Chapter Five

God rescues his own son

Many years later another baby boy had to escape from a wicked ruler. This baby was even more important than King Joash.

The first people to find out that God's *own son* had been born were shepherds. They were delighted that God had told them before he told anybody else.

But other people soon found out as well. Many miles away, clever men were looking at the stars. They saw a special star which meant that someone very important had been born in Israel.

The men were excited. "Let us go and see him!" they said. "He is bound to be a great king."

So they got on their horses and rode off. They travelled for many miles and many days and arrived at Jerusalem. They went straight to the palace because this is where you would expect to find a great king. But when they met the king who lived in the palace, they knew that this was not the right place.

King Herod was jealous and angry. He didn't like the sound of a new king one little bit.

"What!" he shouted to his advisers. "The star means that there is a baby who will rule Israel? I'll never have it! I'm the only king around here. This baby must be got rid of immediately!"

But he told a different story to the men who had travelled so far to find the baby.

So the men set off again. This time they travelled to Bethlehem. King Herod's advisers had told them that the baby was supposed to be born there.

They were delighted, because the star they had seen many months ago was now shining in the sky brighter than ever. It led them all the way to Bethlehem and it even guided them to the house where Jesus was living with Mary and Joseph.

Although Jesus was very young and the house was very small, the men knew at once that they had found their king!

Then the men went home. They were very happy. They did not go back to talk to King Herod because God warned them not to.

But the danger was not over for God's own son. In the middle of the night, Joseph had a terrifying dream!

Even though it was night-time, Joseph got up and woke Mary.

"We must get out of here," he said. "God has told me that King Herod is coming to kill our little boy!"

Sure enough he was right. Because the men who had seen the star had not come back to him, Herod decided to kill all the baby boys who lived in Bethlehem. "That

way I am bound to get rid of this new
King," he said.

Mary wrapped Jesus in a soft blanket
and tied him onto her back with a shawl.

Then Mary and Joseph hurried out into
the night. Soon they left the town of
Bethlehem behind.

Joseph explained that God was sending
them far away from Israel while Herod was
king. "Jesus will never be safe while that
man is on the throne," he said.

And so they walked day after day, mile after mile along the long, hot, dusty road to Egypt.

Some years later, when King Herod died, Joseph and Mary brought Jesus back to Israel again. They went to live in the town of Nazareth and Jesus seemed just an ordinary little boy. Nobody could have guessed then just how important Jesus really was.

If you want to know more about Jesus, the books of Matthew, Mark, Luke and John in the Bible tell the story of his life. This part of Jesus' story is found in Matthew, chapter 2.

Chapter Six

Peter escapes from prison

After Jesus went back to heaven, people started to believe that he was God's son. His friends knew this already, but soon more and more people believed as well.

One of Jesus' friends, called Peter, loved telling others about Jesus. "God will forgive you for all the wrong things you have done, if you tell Jesus that you are sorry," he said.

God did amazing things through Peter, to prove that what he was saying was true. Many people were healed.

But the leaders of the people in Jerusalem did not like what was happening. They knew that if people started to follow Jesus, they would stop following them. So they decided to put Peter in prison. They were even wondering whether to kill him.

The night before Peter was to be brought to trial, he was sitting in a gloomy prison cell. Peter was chained to two huge soldiers and he was fast asleep. Suddenly...

It was an angel! Peter stood up and the

chains fell from his feet and his wrists.
"Grab your clothes and follow me," said
the angel.

The angel headed for the door, which
opened by itself. Peter thought he was
dreaming. The guards seemed to see
nothing. The next door opened by itself as
well. Then they reached the main gate of
the prison that led to the city. This gate
was made of iron. It was as wide as it was
high. There was a massive creak and then...

The next thing Peter knew, he was outside in the fresh air. He walked away from the prison with the angel, as quickly as he could.

But when Peter looked around – the angel was gone! Peter shook himself. "I wasn't dreaming," he said. "This is real. God has sent his angel to rescue me from prison. I'm as free as a bird!"

Peter laughed. "Thank you, God!" he said. Then he hurried off to a friend's house. Many people who were followers of Jesus had gathered there to pray. They were all praying for Peter because they were so worried about him!

"Oh please Lord, rescue Peter!" cried one.

"Yes, do something, Jesus!" cried another. "We don't want Peter to be killed tomorrow morning."

Just then, a servant girl heard someone knocking at the door.

The servant girl was so delighted when she heard Peter's voice that she rushed in to tell the others straight away. She forgot to open the door for Peter! He was left standing out in the cold, with a locked door in front of him.

Back inside, nobody believed the servant girl. "It can't be Peter," they said. "Peter's locked in prison. You must be hearing things."

The servant girl kept on saying, "It *is* him. I know his voice."

Peter kept on knocking. At last, after a long while, someone else went to the door and opened it. Imagine their surprise! Peter was standing there, looking rather grumpy.

The whole room burst into cheers. Peter came in. He was grinning now. "Shush!" he cried. "You don't want the whole city to know that I am here."

Then, he told them the whole story...

If you want to find out more about Peter, this story can be found in Acts, chapter 12.

Chapter Seven

Paul is saved from the sea

Paul was another follower of Jesus. He was also put in prison many times for telling people how wonderful Jesus was.

One day Paul was sent as a prisoner on a ship to Rome. At first, it was not too bad because the army officer who had been put in charge of Paul was a kind man. His name was Julius.

But after many days at sea, a storm began to blow. The wind tossed the ship in every direction and the rain poured down. At last, the sailors gave up trying to steer the ship at all. They just let it go wherever it wanted to go.

The sailors were frightened. They had never seen a storm like this before. The sky was black with thunder clouds. In the daytime there was no sun and at night there were no stars. No-one knew exactly where the ship was, but they all knew that they were miles from where they wanted to be.

Everyone felt miserable. Everyone felt scared. And everyone felt very, very seasick.

But down in his little corner of the big cabin next to the hold, Paul was praying. "Please Lord, will you help us?" he was saying. "Please Lord, will you have mercy on this ship and its crew?" He prayed on and on, into the night.

Then one morning just before daybreak, Paul came up on to the deck. The ship looked terrible. Most of the mast was gone, the sails were torn and the rudder was broken. They had been in the storm for fourteen days. Paul spoke to the captain and the crew.

"Don't give up!" he said. "God has told me that we are not going to drown. We are going to be washed up on some island and we will all be saved." The men could hardly believe it. It seemed too good to be true.

Paul continued talking. "You should eat something," he said. "You will need all the energy you can get!"

Everyone felt better after what Paul had said. They all joined Paul and had some breakfast.

As the daylight got brighter, someone cried, "I can see land!"

And sure enough, there it was. Then they all heard a terrible crunching sound as the ship hit the seabed of the sea near the coast.

"We'll have to swim for it!" said Paul. "The ship is breaking up!"

They all jumped into the water as the ship was falling to pieces around them.

Although they were still quite a long way from the land, they all reached the beach safely!

Then local people came to help them. They had landed on an island called Malta and the people were very friendly. The people of the island made a fire, to help the shipwrecked men get warm. Paul helped as well. He was just carrying a bunch of sticks to the fire when...

"He's bound to die!" cried a man from the island. "Those snakes are poisonous, you know!"

Paul shook the snake off into the fire. Everybody waited, but nothing happened to Paul.

"It takes more than a shipwreck and a poisonous snake to stop him!" laughed Julius. "This man is on a mission from God!" The islanders looked interested.

"Shall I tell you what I know about God?" said Paul.

"Yes!" said the islanders.

And so Paul began... He told them all about Jesus and they were *very* interested.

God had lots of work for Paul to do on that island. Many people were healed and many people found out about Jesus. Paul stayed there for three months. After that he set off for Rome in a new ship!

If you want to find out more about Paul and the shipwreck, the story can be found in Acts, chapters 27 and 28.

Some more books to enjoy!

Hidden Heroes of the Bible

Clio Turner

Many people in the Bible did wonderful things for God. Some of these people are less well known. This book tells the stories of Miriam, who was a brave sister, Deborah who went to war, Gideon who was a most unlikely leader, Philip and Barnabas and others.

Read their exciting stories in this new book!

ISBN 1 85999 434 2.
Price £3.50

**Available from your local Christian bookshop, or online at
www.scriptureunion.org.uk/publishing
or call Mail Order direct on 01908 856006**

Bernard Bunting
The Missing
Birthday
Ro Willoughby

Bernard's birthday
seems to have been
forgotten in the
excitement of preparing
for Christmas – or so Bernard thinks. Does
God know about this and does he care?
Bernard is in for a big surprise.

ISBN 1 85999 327 3
Price £3.50

Available from your local Christian bookshop,
or online at
www.scriptureunion.org.uk/publishing
or call Mail Order direct on 01908 856006

Tales of Young Maximus Mouse
Brian Ogden

"Do you remember that day at school when we swapped the cheese for plasticine?" asked Maximus. "Too right," said Mick. "All the mouselings and teachers picked up the plasticine and took a big bite. It was a pity they caught us though! We missed our playtimes for a whole week." Maximus Mouse lets us into the secrets of his life as a mouseling.

ISBN 1 85999 328 1
Price £3.50

Available from your local Christian bookshop, or online at www.scriptureunion.org.uk/publishing or call Mail Order direct on 01908 856006